GW01458557

www.wrote.be

WELCOME TO THE WORLD OF TRACTORS

Dear little explorers,
you're about to start **an incredible adventure!** Imagine entering a world where **huge machines with giant wheels** work tirelessly in fields, forests, and even in the snow. These are **tractors, the true heroes of work!**

There are tractors that work in orchards, picking apples and oranges, and others that climb mountains to help farmers. In this book, we'll discover all the secrets of these gentle giants.
We'll see how they work, what jobs they do, and why they're so important for all of us. Are you ready to hop on board and start this exciting journey?
BUCKLE UP, LET'S GO!

A tractor is like a **superhero of the fields!** It's a big, strong vehicle with **huge wheels** that can cross mud and hills. It makes a deep noise: *'VROOM, VROOM!'*

Tractors are **very strong.** They can pull extremely heavy loads and work for hours without getting tired. They are the farmers' best friends and help us produce the food we eat every day.

WHAT IS A TRACTOR?

THE CABIN

The most important part is **the cabin.** *It's like a little house on wheels* where the driver sits. From there, they can see everything and control the tractor. There are many buttons and levers that look difficult, but for a skilled driver, *they're as easy as playing a video game!*

THE BIG WHEELS

Tractor wheels are enormous, taller than many children! **These giant wheels have an important job.** They help the tractor move on difficult terrain without sinking. The bigger the wheels, the better the tractor can work in muddy or bumpy fields. *Some wheels have special designs, like big teeth, that help the tractor not to slip.* The back wheels are often bigger than the front ones, to give the tractor more power when pulling heavy equipment.

SO MUCH POWER

Tractors are very powerful machines. Their engine is like a big heart beating strongly. A tractor's strength is measured in "horsepower", but they're not real horses! A big tractor can have the strength of *hundreds of horses*. This power helps the tractor pull heavy tools and work all day long.

THE AUTONOMOUS DRIVING

Modern tractors are like **giant computers on wheels!** Some can drive themselves, without a farmer at the wheel.

These special tractors use satellites in space to know exactly where they are in the field. It's as if they had a magic map of the sky!

With cameras and sensors, smart tractors see everything around them. *They can avoid obstacles and follow perfect paths, without missing even by a centimeter.* Autonomous tractors work day and night, helping farmers grow more food. They can plant seeds, water plants, and harvest fruits, **all by themselves!** These tractors of the future show us how technology can make farming easier and more efficient. It's like having a robotic helper in the fields!

WHAT CAN IT DO?

Behind the cabin, tractors have special attachments. They're like the tractor's hands and can hook up many different tools. With these tools, a tractor can plow fields, sow seeds, harvest crops, and do many other jobs.

But tractors don't only work in fields. There are tractors that clear snow from roads in winter, others that move big trees in forests, and even small tractors that mow grass in parks!

FROM FIELD TO TABLE

Our tractor friends don't just work in the fields! They're part of a big adventure that brings food from farms to our tables. *Let's discover together how tractors help us in every step of this magical journey!*

The gentle giants prepare the Soil

In spring, the big green tractors prepare the fields. The plow tractor digs long furrows, as if it were drawing on a huge brown sheet.

Then the harrow makes the soil smooth and soft. Finally, the seeder spreads the seeds, as if it were putting them to bed. These gentle giants work all day in the field. *Thanks to them, the seeds grow and become the food we eat.*

THE TRACTORS ADVENTURE

Growing Healthy and Strong

As the little plants grow, they need lots of care, just like children. The tractors become like babysitters for *the vegetables!* Tractors help the plants grow. Some bring water, others give special food to the plants, carefully passing between the rows.

Day by day, the little plants grow bigger and bigger. Finally, the most exciting moment arrives: **the harvest!** Big machines called combine harvesters enter the field. They look like friendly dragons that eat the ripe plants and collect the fruits and grains. *It's like a big harvest party!*

After the harvest, tractors load the food onto big trucks. The trucks carry fruits, vegetables, and grains from farms to cities. The food arrives at shops and markets, where people buy it.

The Journey of the Harvest

Finally, the food reaches our tables. When you eat, think about the long journey of the food. Remember the work of tractors and farmers that made it possible.

Let's Discover the World of TRACTORS!

Have you ever thought about how many different types of tractors exist? There are tractors of every shape and size! *Some are giants that work in big fields. Others are small and nimble, perfect for moving between fruit trees. There are tractors that can climb mountains and others that clean beaches. In the next pages, we'll meet many special tractors. We'll discover what they do and why they're so important. Get ready for an adventure full of giant wheels, powerful engines, and amazing jobs!*

Are you ready to meet these incredible helpers?

FIELD TRACTOR

The field tractor is like a big green friend for farmers. It has huge wheels and a powerful engine that allow it to work in large fields. This tractor can plow the soil, plant seeds, and help plants grow. **It's EVERY FARMER'S BEST FRIEND!**

DID YOU KNOW?

A big tractor can have wheels taller than three children standing on top of each other?

Some modern tractors have air conditioning and radio in the cabin, just like a car.

The biggest tractor in the world is as tall as a two-story house and weighs as much as 16 elephants!

The first tractors were steam-powered and looked like big locomotives moving in the fields.

If we lined up all the tractors in the world, we could circle the Earth several times!

Some tractors can "talk" to each other using special computers, deciding together how to take care of the field.

FIELD TRACTOR

THE COMBINE HARVESTER

The combine harvester is like a huge friendly dragon that devours entire fields of wheat, corn, or rice. **This impressive machine does the work of many in a single pass: it cuts the plants, separates the grains, and collects them.** As tall as a house and as wide as a truck, the combine harvester is the star of the show during harvest time.

THE GIANT OF THE HARVEST

The combine harvester is a real mobile factory. Here's how this amazing machine works:

First, its big front "mouth", called the cutting bar, cuts the mature plants. **Then, inside the machine, the plants are threshed to make all the grains fall out.** A system of sieves and fans separates the good grains from the straw and chaff. The grains are collected in a large tank, while the straw is expelled from the back of the machine.

THE COMBINE HARVESTER

When the tank is full, the combine can unload the grains into a truck or trailer without stopping, like an airplane refueling in flight! *Modern combines have computers and GPS that help them work with great precision, ensuring that not even a single grain is wasted.*

DID YOU KNOW?

A modern combine harvester can collect more than 100 tons of grain in an hour, enough to make over 300,000 sandwiches!

Some combine harvesters have such powerful lights that they can work even at night.

The cabin of a modern combine is as comfortable as a luxury car, with air conditioning and touch-screen computers.

There are special combines for harvesting tomatoes, peas, and even blueberries!

The world's largest combine harvester is as wide as 8 cars lined up.

Before the invention of combine harvesters, it took weeks to harvest by hand the same amount of grain that can now be harvested in just a few hours.

THE COMBINE HARVESTER

THE BALER TRACTOR

The baler tractor is like a big chef that prepares food for farm animals. It collects grass and straw from the fields and turns them into large rolls, which look like huge cinnamon rolls. These rolls are food for cows, horses, and sheep when grass doesn't grow.

The baler tractor does a very special job. First, it collects the cut grass or straw from the field. Then, it spins it round and round inside a machine called a baler, which rolls it up very tightly.

When the roll is big enough, the machine wraps it with a net or string. It's like making a big round sandwich for the animals!

After the bales are made, another tractor with a special arm picks them up and stacks them. These bales are stored for winter, when grass doesn't grow in the fields.
The baler tractor helps farmers prepare lots of food for animals in a short time. It's like a superhero making sure cows, horses, and sheep always have something to eat!

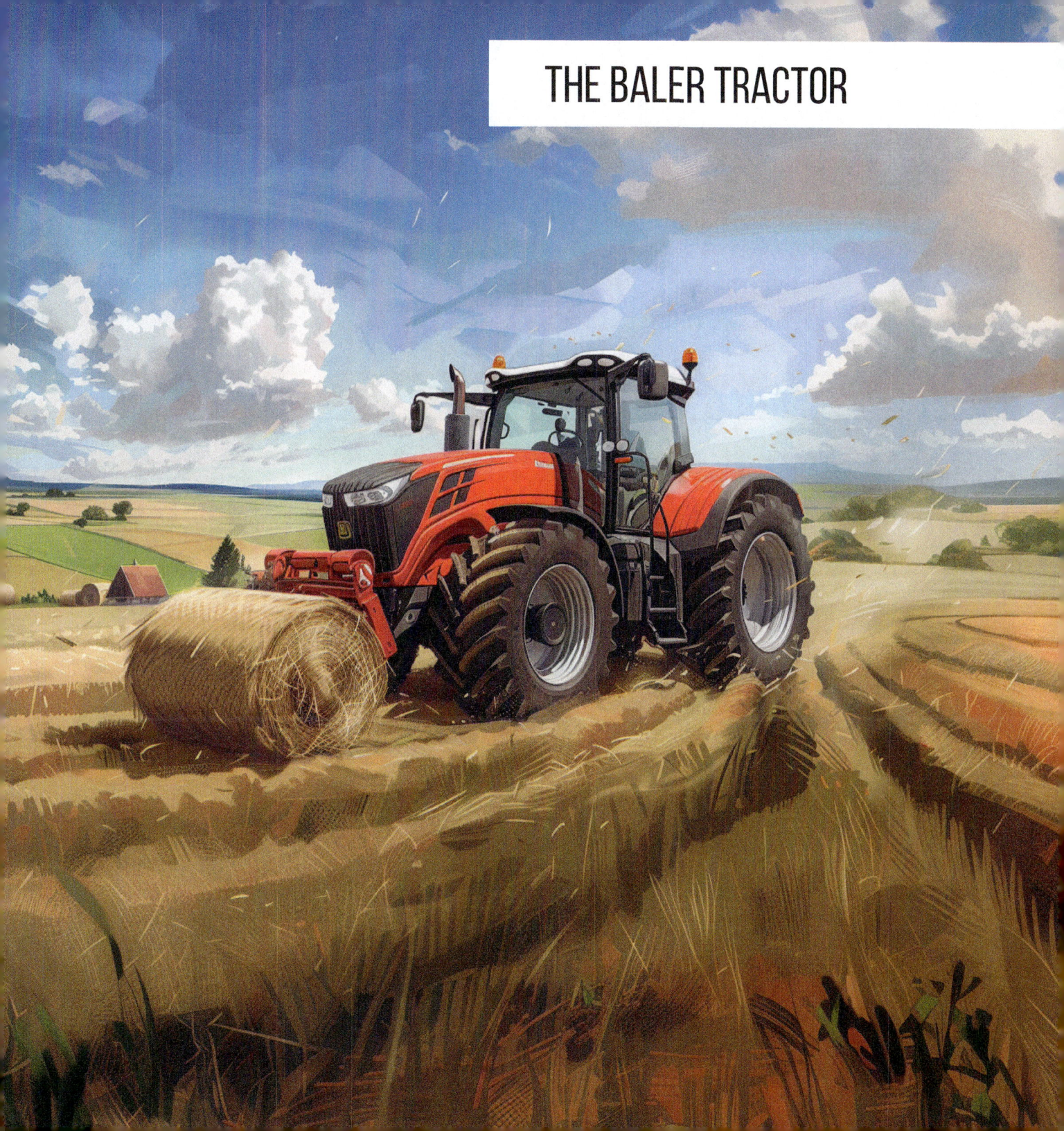

THE BALER TRACTOR

DID YOU KNOW?

A bale can be as big as a small car!

If we stacked all the bales made in a year on top of each other, we could reach the moon!

Some baler tractors can make square bales instead of round ones.

Bales are sometimes wrapped in colored plastic and look like huge candies in the fields.

In some countries, they have competitions to see who can roll a bale the farthest.

Some artists use bales to make giant sculptures that look like animals or funny monsters.

THE BALER TRACTOR

THE VINEYARD TRACTOR

The vineyard tractor is a little hero that dances between the vines. It's low and narrow, so it can move between the rows of grapes without touching the bunches. This special tractor helps grow the grapes that will become juice or wine. It's the best friend of grape growers!

AN AGILE DANCER

The vineyard tractor does many things to help the grapes grow. It sprays water on the leaves to keep them clean and healthy. It feeds the vines by spreading special food called fertilizer. This tractor also cuts the grass between the rows of vines. When it's time to harvest the grapes, it helps by carrying baskets to put the bunches in.

It can work on steep hills without falling over. Some modern tractors even have arms that help pick the grapes!

DID YOU KNOW?

Some vineyard tractors are so narrow they could pass through a house door!

In some very steep vineyards, tractors have tracks instead of wheels to avoid slipping.

There are vineyard tractors that can tilt to the side to work better on slopes.

Some of these tractors have swivel seats, so the driver can look both forward and backward without turning around.

The world's smallest vineyard tractor is only 1 meter wide, less than the length of a bed!

THE SNOWPLOW TRACTOR

The snowplow tractor is like a superhero that fights against snow. It has a big blade in front that pushes snow away from the roads. This special tractor helps people move around when there's a lot of snow. It's everyone's friend in winter, making the roads safe for going to school or shopping!

THE WINTER KNIGHT

THE SNOWPLOW TRACTOR

The snowplow tractor has a very important job in winter. When it snows a lot, it goes out to clear the roads. Its big blade pushes the snow to the side, making a path for cars and people.

Some snowplow tractors also have a salt spreader. They throw salt on the road to keep it from getting slippery. It's like they're laying down a magic non-slip carpet! These tractors often work at night or very early in the morning. So, when we wake up, we find the roads already cleared for going to school or work. Snowplow tractors are very strong. They can push away a lot of snow in a short time. They are the silent heroes of winter!

DID YOU KNOW?

The blade of a big snowplow tractor can be as wide as three cars lined up!

Some snowplow tractors have flashing colored lights, like moving Christmas trees.

There are snowplow tractors that can throw snow very far, as if they were having a giant snowball fight.

At some airports, they use giant snowplow tractors to clean the runways for airplanes.

Some snowplow tractors have special cameras to see well even when there's a lot of snow falling.

The salt these tractors spread is like the salt we use in the kitchen, but bigger.

THE SNOW CAT

The Snow Cat is a very special tractor that loves to play in the snow and on ice. It has huge tracks instead of wheels, which allow it to move on deep snow without sinking.

This brave tractor helps prepare ski slopes and keep mountain roads open during winter. It can climb steep slopes and cross snow fields where other vehicles would stop. The Snow Cat also works at night, with powerful headlights that light up its path. It's like a winter superhero, making the mountains safe and fun for everyone!

ORCHARD TRACTOR

The orchard tractor is a true champion of agility! **Small and slim, this special tractor moves gracefully between rows of fruit trees.** With its compact shape, it can pass under branches loaded with apples, pears, or oranges without damaging them. It's like a dancer in the agricultural world, ready to take care of each tree with precision and gentleness.

DID YOU KNOW?

Some of these tractors have seats that fold sideways to allow the driver to see better under the branches.

There are orchard tractors that can change the width of their wheels to adapt to different types of trees.

Some modern models have pressurized cabins to protect the driver from the sprays used on the trees.

The smallest orchard tractors weigh less than a car!

In some countries, they use orchard tractors to harvest olives from trees.

THE TANK TRACTOR

The tank tractor is like a giant watering can on wheels.
It has a big tank full of water on its back. This special tractor helps give water to plants in large fields. It's every farmer's friend when it doesn't rain enough!

THE TRACKED TRACTOR

The tracked tractor is like a peaceful tank that conquers difficult terrain. Instead of wheels, it has "ribbons" called tracks that allow it to move on mud, snow, and slippery ground without sinking. **Sturdy and powerful, this special tractor can work where others would stop, bravely facing the toughest challenges in the fields.**

THE MUD WARRIOR

The tracked tractor is a true champion of working in tough conditions. **Its tracks spread the weight over a larger area, allowing it to "float" on terrain where other tractors would sink.** In very muddy fields, like rice paddies, the tracked tractor moves easily, preparing the ground for planting. On steep slopes, it maintains a firm grip, working safely where normal wheels would slip.

In winter, when snow covers the fields, the tracked tractor keeps working, opening paths and moving large amounts of snow. These tractors are also very useful in forestry work, moving nimbly between trees on rough terrain. *Some models can even swim, crossing small streams!*

FORESTRY TRACTOR

The forestry tractor is like a great forest explorer. It's strong and sturdy, built to move among tall trees and on difficult terrain. This special tractor helps move large logs and take care of the forest.

It's the friend of all lumberjacks and helps keep the woods healthy and tidy!

BEACH CLEANER TRACTOR

The beach cleaner tractor is like a big comb that cleans the sand. This special tractor passes over the beach and collects trash, seaweed, and other objects that shouldn't be there. It helps keep beaches clean and safe for all of us who want to play and swim. *It's like a superhero that saves beaches!*

LAWN MOWER TRACTOR

The lawn mower tractor is like a big hairdresser for grass.
This special tractor cuts the grass to make lawns beautiful and tidy. It has blades under its belly that spin quickly and cut the grass like many scissors. It's the favorite of those who take care of parks, golf courses, and large gardens!

A SPECIAL GOODBYE

Dear little explorers of the tractor world,

Our journey is about to end, but the adventure continues in fields, orchards, and farms all around the world. Remember, every tractor you see from now on has a story to tell and an important job to do. Maybe one day you'll be the one driving these gentle giants, inventing new ones, or tending the fields they care for with so much love. *Thank you for traveling with us through the wonderful world of tractors. Now, every time you see a golden field, a lush orchard, or a well-tended lawn, you'll know there's a tractor hero behind all that beauty.*

Goodbye, and remember: the future is like an open field, ready to be explored.

What tracks will your tractor leave?

LEAVE A REVIEW

WRO TE.BE

To help us grow, your words are incredibly precious to us and to help other children discover this fantastic world of tractors.

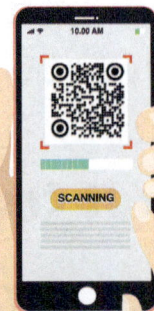

WRO TE.BE CLUB

DOWNLOAD EXTRA
HERE ARE YOUR SPECIAL CONTENTS
a gift for you

Yes, that's right! We've prepared it for you.
Getting the special content is easy.
Follow these instructions:

Visit the site: Open your browser and go to the page

wrote.be/en/club

Enter the Code:
You'll find a field where you can enter the following exclusive code:

4099E

This code was created especially for book owners and will give you access to a bonus with unique resources that you can download directly to your device.

Printed in Great Britain
by Amazon